Mein Trump

America's Favorite Fascist in His Own Words

by

Atticus X

"Jeb Bush has to like the Mexican illegals because of his wife."

(deleted Twitter post, 2015)

"If Hillary Clinton can't satisfy her husband what makes her think she can satisfy America?"

(Twitter 4/16/15)

"You know, it doesn't really matter what [the media] write as long as you've got a young and beautiful piece of ass."

(Esquire 1991)

"26,000 unreported sexual assaults in the military-only 238 convictions.

What did these guys expect when they put men and women together?"

(Twitter 5/7/13)

"LOOK AT THAT FACE! WOULD ANYONE VOTE FOR THAT? CAN YOU IMAGINE THAT, THE FACE OF OUR NEXT PRESIDENT?"

(ON CARLY FIORINA, 9/15 ROLLING STONE)

"I think apologizing's a great thing, but you have to be wrong. I will absolutely

apologize, sometime in the hopefully distant future, if I'm ever wrong."

(On The Tonight Show Starring Jimmy Fallon 9/15)

"You haven't been called, go back to Univision."

(to Latino reporter Jorge Ramos at an Iowa rally in 8/15)

"YOU COULD SEE THERE WAS BLOOD COMING OUT OF HER EYES. BLOOD COMING OUT OF HER... WHEREVER."

(ON FOX NEWS HOST MEGYN KELLY DURING A CNN INTERVIEW 8/15)

"He's not a war hero. He's a war hero because he was captured?

I like people who weren't captured."

(On John McCain at a Family Leadership Summit 7/15)

"When Mexico sends its people, they're not sending the best. They're sending

people that have lots of problems and they're bringing those problems.

They're bringing drugs, they're bringing crime. They're rapists and some, I assume,

are good people, but I speak to border guards

and they're telling us what we're getting."

(Referring to Mexicans during a speech announcing his presidential candidacy in 6/15)

"NBC News just called it 'The Great Freeze' — coldest weather in years.

Is our country still spending money on the global warming hoax?"

(Twitter 2014)

"I have a great relationship with the blacks. I've always

had a great relationship with the blacks."

(On Albany's Talk Radio 1300 in 4/11)

"I've said if Ivanka weren't my daughter, perhaps I'd be dating her."

(Commenting on *his daughter* on The View 2006)

"Sorry losers and haters, but my I.Q. is one of the highest -and you all know it! Please don't feel so stupid or insecure, it's not your fault."

(Twitter 5/13)

"I will be the greatest jobs president that God has ever created."

(At Trump Towers 6/15)

'How Stupid Are the People of Iowa?"

(National Review 11/15)

"PEOPLE LOVE ME. AND YOU KNOW WHAT, I HAVE BEEN VERY SUCCESSFUL. EVERYBODY LOVES ME."

(FOX 13, UT. 3/13)

"The point is that you can't be too greedy."

(From the book "The Art of the Deal")

"The wall will go up and Mexico will start behaving."

(Bill O'Reilly 6/15)

"Sadly, because president Obama has done such a poor job as president, you won't see another black president for generations!"

(Twitter 11/14)

"Because I don't want to, Greta."

(On sharing his secret plan to destroy ISIS with the president on Greta Van Susteren)

"There should be a total and complete shutdown' of Muslims entering the United States."

(Speaking on the USS Yorktown)

"Black guys counting my money! I hate it. The only kind of people I want counting my money are little short guys that wear yarmulkes every day."

(Rolling Stone 6/15)

"Look, we can bring the American Dream back. That I will tell you. We're bringing it back. OK? And I understand what you're saying. And I get that from so many people. "Is The American Dream dead?" They are asking me the

question, "Is the American Dream dead?" And the

American Dream is in trouble. That I can tell you. OK? It's in trouble. But we're going to get it back and do some real jobs."

(Rochester Town Hall Meeting 9/15)

"One of the key problems today is that politics is such a disgrace. Good people don't go into government."

(The Advocate, 2000)

"I could stand in the middle of Fifth Avenue and shoot somebody and I wouldn't lose any voters, okay?"

(Sioux Center, Iowa 1/2016)

A response to Don Lemon (CNN) about his infamous Mexican comments:

"Well, somebody' s doing the raping, Don. I mean somebody' s doing it!"

Why do the networks continue to put dopey Bill Kristol on panels when he has called every single shot about me wrong for 2 yrs?

(Twitter 5/22/2016)

"I like Michael Douglas!" (Twitter 5/17/2016)

"All of the women on 'The Apprentice' flirted with me — consciously or unconsciously. That's to be expected." — How To Get Rich, 2004

"You mean Pocahontas?" Trump said to New York Times columnist Maureen Dowd, in reference to Massachusetts Sen. Elizabeth Warren (D).

"All of the men, we're petrified to speak to women anymore. We may raise our voice. You know what? The women get it better than we do, folks. They get it better than we do. If she didn't play that card, she has nothing." — on Hillary Clinton and the "women's card" at a campaign rally in Spokane, Washington, in May 2016

"Happy #CincoDeMayo! The best taco bowls are made in Trump Tower Grill. I love Hispanics!" (Twitter 5/5/2016)

"We can't continue to allow China to rape our country" — on America's trade deficit with China.

"I think the only card she has is the women's card," Trump said of Hillary Clinton's presidential campaign. "She has got nothing else going. Frankly, if Hillary Clinton were a man, I don't think she would get 5% of the vote. And the beautiful thing is, women don't like her."

"Look at those hands. Are they small hands? And [Republican candidate Marco Rubio] referred to my hands — if they're small, something else must be small. I guarantee you there's no problem, I guarantee." — *on his penis.*

"Our great African-American President hasn't exactly had a positive impact on the thugs who are so happily and openly destroying Baltimore."

(On protests after the death of Freddie Gray)

On November 6, 2012, Donald Trump tweeted: "The concept of global warming was created by and for the Chinese in order to make U.S. manufacturing non-competitive."

"I love the poorly educated."

(2/2016)

On gay marriage May 11, 2016:

"It's like in golf. A lot of people -- I don't want this to sound trivial -- but a lot of people are switching to these really long putters, very unattractive. It's weird. You see these great players with these really long putters, because they can't sink three-footers anymore. And, I hate it. I am a traditionalist. I have so many fabulous friends who happen to be gay, but I am a traditionalist."

During September 2015 GOP Debate:

"I am totally in favor of vaccines. But I want smaller doses over a longer period of time. Same exact amount, but you take this little beautiful baby, and you pump--I mean, it looks just like it's meant for a horse, not for a child, and we've had so many instances, people that work for me. ... [in which] a child, a beautiful child went to have the vaccine, and came back and a week later had a tremendous fever, got very, very sick, now is autistic."

March 2011 on ABC's Good Morning America

"Part of the beauty of me is that I am very rich."

Heil Trump!